THE BEST EVER JOBS

JOBS IN

SCIENCE

PAUL MASON

PowerKiDS press™

NEW YORK

Published in 2023 by The Rosen Publishing Group, Inc.
29 East 21st Street, New York, NY 10010

Series editor: Amy Pimperton
Produced by Tall Tree Ltd
Editor: Lara Murphy
Designer: Gary Hyde

Cataloging-in-Publication Data
Names: Mason, Paul.
Title: Jobs in science / Paul Mason.
Description: New York : PowerKids Press, 2023. | Series: The best ever jobs
| Includes glossary and index.
Identifiers: ISBN 9781725339194 (pbk.) | ISBN 9781725339200 (library
bound) | ISBN 9781725339217 (ebook)
Subjects: LCSH: Science--Vocational guidance--Juvenile literature.
Classification: LCC Q147.M376 2023 | DDC 502.3--dc23

Picture Credits
t-top, b-bottom, l-left, r-right, c-centre, front cover-fc, back cover - bc
3tl, 5r, 20l, 21r, 22–23 and 46br shutterstock/Julia Waller, 3tr, 4tr and 4r shutterstock/Picture Window,
3r, 5r, 5l, 9t and 46bl shutterstock/StockSmartStart, 3bl, 4br, 18b and 19tr shutterstock/bsd, 3br and 19c
shutterstock/Vadim Almiev, 4tl shutterstock/Iconic Bestiary, 4c, 8l, 10tl, 13b, 14, 25c, 32cr, 43t and 46tr
shutterstock/lineartestpilot, 4cl and 37tr shutterstock/AlfaSmart, 4bl shutterstock/Evgeny Turaev, 5tr
shutterstock/Black creator 24,6l and 15t shutterstock/Pretty Vectors, 7t shutterstock/Melok, 7b
shutterstock/Twocoms,8r and 47br shutterstock/vector_brothers, 9r tksteven, 10b shutterstock/owatta,
11c shutterstock/muuraa, 11b shutterstock/PRESSLAB, 12l shutterstock/Aayam 4D, 12b shutterstock/
Visual Generation, 13t shutterstock/GoodStudio, 13l shutterstocl/Anna Rassadnikova, 13br
shutterstock/LSpirov, 15bc Marc Lieberman,15br National Cancer Institute, 16bl shutterstock/
BigMouse, 16br shutterstock/LongQuattro, 17t shutterstock/K N, 17br shutterstock/LightField Studios,
18r shutterstock/graphicwithart, 19b Eric Drexler, 20br shutterstock/Anetlanda, 21tr Thea Boodhoo,
22b shutterstock/paleontologist natural, 25t shutterstock/MasterGraph, 25br University of Chicago
Photographic Archive, apf1-03867, Special Collections Research Center, University of Chicago Library,
27t shutterstock/Marina Sun, 27br briola Giancarlo edp, 28b shutterstock/D-VISIONS, 29tr
shutterstock/alllikeballoon, 29bl Brookhaven National Laboratory, 30l shutterstock/Studio Photo MH,
30bl shutterstock/Oleksandr Panasovskyi, 30b shutterstocj/adecvatman, 31tl shutterstock/Lal Perera,
31br shutterstock/Gorodenkoff, 32b shutterstock/Aluna1, 33br shutterstock/Maquiladora, 34cl
shutterstock/Set Line Vector Icon, 34bl shutterstock/bessyana, 35tl shutterstock/FMStox, 35br
shutterstock/Golden Sikorka, 36 shutterstock/Ficus777, 37b Felice Frankel, 38l and 39tl shutterstock/
owatta, 38b shutterstock/Panda Vector, 39tl shutterstock/Helen Lane, 39b and 45br NASA, 40
shutterstock/Bodor Tivadar, 41t shutterstock/Mika Besfamilnaya, 41tr NOAA, 41b shutterstock/
shaineast, 42l and 44 shutterstock/Padma Sanjaya, 42r shutterstock/Anastasiia Sorokina, 43br Biswarup
Ganguly, 45tl shutterstock/Art studio G.

Every attempt has been made to clear copyright. Should there be any inadvertent omission, please
apply to the publisher for rectification. The facts, dates and statistics in this book were correct at the
time of printing.

Manufactured in the United States of America

CPSIA Compliance Information: Batch #CSPK23. For further information contact Rosen Publishing, New York, New York at 1-800-237-9932.

Find us on

Contents

Top science jobs

You might think science is all about test tubes, microscopes, and wearing a white lab coat, but think again. Scientists are just as likely to go to work wearing a heatproof suit, hard hat, wetsuit, or even a spacesuit. Studying science could open up lots of amazing jobs in areas you might not have thought of before. Here are just a few:

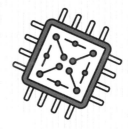

SPORTS

Imagine developing a fitness program for one of the top football teams, helping the members of an international cycling squad work out a way to pedal better, or working on clothing that will help race-car drivers stay cool in the cockpit. Sports scientists do all these things and many more.

CRIMINOLOGY

The first person allowed to investigate the scene of a major crime isn't the detective—it's a scientist. He or she is a forensic investigator, there to gather evidence of what happened. Each year, forensic evidence helps put many criminals behind bars.

SPACE

Have you ever thought you'd like to visit space? Then you'd better hit the science books! To join an astronaut program, you must have studied biological, physical, or computer science, engineering, or mathematics in college. Almost everyone aboard the International Space Station (ISS) is a scientist.

PALEONTOLOGY

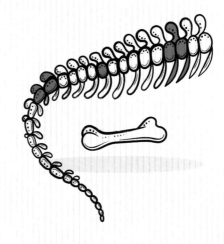

Paleontology—the study of fossils, including dinosaur fossils—is jammed with scientists. Paleontologists calculate how old rocks are, work out how dinosaurs walked or what kind of feathers they had, and investigate the plants, landscapes, and climate of the prehistoric world.

Astronomer

The night sky is filled with amazing objects, including twinkling stars, distant planets, and glowing clouds of gas. If staring at stars fascinates you, then perhaps you could be cut out for a career in astronomy, where the sky is quite literally the limit!

STUDYING SPACE

Many astronomers get to use some of the most powerful telescopes ever built. These could be located on tall mountains or even out in orbit where they get a clear view of space. As well as observing the night sky, you will pour over data and photos, trying to interpret events that occurred millions of light-years away.

UNIVERSE WONDERS

There are many branches to astronomy and specializing in a particular field could see you hunting for alien planets around distant stars, studying strange galaxies at the edge of the cosmos, or even trying to find new and exotic particles that could help us explain how the universe came into existence. You could end up controlling the actions of a space telescope in orbit or studying the effects of strange particles deep within our planet.

A degree in a STEM subject, including math and physics, will propel you on a career to studying comets, planets, stars, galaxies, and even black holes.

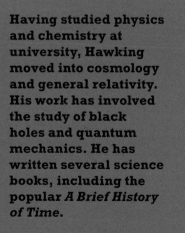

STEM STAR: STEPHEN HAWKING
(1942-2018)

Having studied physics and chemistry at university, Hawking moved into cosmology and general relativity. His work has involved the study of black holes and quantum mechanics. He has written several science books, including the popular *A Brief History of Time*.

Astronaut

Imagine seeing Earth from somewhere only a few other people have ever seen it, over 60 miles (100 km) above the surface. You'd be inside a small spacecraft that is surrounded by the airless vacuum of space and lots of dangerous radiation. If that sounds exciting, perhaps you could become an astronaut.

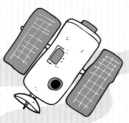

SPACE WORK

Astronauts have all kinds of jobs to do in space. On a space station they perform science experiments, including experiments on themselves to find out how their bodies change in space. These experiments help us work out whether humans could one day live in space. Astronauts also have to do everyday "housework" jobs: cooking, keeping their spacecraft clean, and repairing any problems.

Astronauts need all kinds of surprising skills. For example, because most astronauts leave Earth through Russian territory, they need to be able to speak Russian for communications.

???!

ERR... HELLO!

SPACE SPECIALISTS

There are two key types of astronauts. Flight specialists manage the flight of spacecraft. This could be its flight from and to Earth, or it could be the position of a space station. The flight commander is the most senior astronaut and is in charge. Mission specialists each have a particular job to do. These might include science research, going on space walks, being in charge of food and drink, or docking with other spacecraft.

STEM STAR: LIU YANG (1978-)

In China, Liu Yang is sometimes called the "Flying Knight." Having trained to fly planes, she was noted for staying calm even when one of her plane engines was disabled! After being recruited into China's space program, Liu Yang became China's first woman to enter space in 2012.

Crime-scene Investigator

Your favorite top has gone missing! You immediately seal the area and begin an investigation. After a careful search, you find the top hidden under a pile of clothes in your brother or sister's room. If that sounds like you, then you're a natural **crime-scene investigator.**

FIRST ON THE SCENE

Before even the detectives are allowed near a crime scene, specialist evidence gatherers seal off the area and go in. The investigators label important items, then photograph everything so that they have a record of exactly where everything was. They look for and collect evidence left behind that shows who was there and how the events happened. The detectives can then use this evidence to work out who committed the crime.

WORLD OF EVIDENCE

There are lots of different types of evidence at crime scenes, so investigators may specialize in one particular kind. Some are experts at crime-scene photography. Others gather forensic evidence, such as blood, saliva, footprints, or tire marks. Crime-scene investigators also gather fingerprints from victims and from the scene. Whatever they do, the investigators must record everything carefully, in as much detail as possible.

TRAINING:
CRIME-SCENE PHOTOGRAPHER

Most crime-scene photographers go to a school to study photography. There they gain knowledge about the specialist skills needed at crimes scenes. These include lighting, the correct order in which to photograph crimes, infrared photography, photographing fingerprints, and handling special chemicals they may need to use.

A crime-scene photographer carefully gathers evidence.

Behind the scenes:
Famous investigations

Crime-scene investigators have been helping solve difficult cases for over a century. The material they gather is used in chemical tests, fingerprint and DNA analysis, and blood typing. This kind of forensic evidence has been important since the early 1800s.

THE ARSENIC TEST

In the 1700s, a deadly poison called arsenic was known as "inheritance powder." It could not be detected: if one wanted to murder an elderly relative and inherit all their money, all they had to do was put arsenic in their tea. Then, in 1832, the chemist James Marsh designed a test for arsenic poisoning. The science of toxicology was born, and arsenic quickly went out of fashion among murderers.

FINGERPRINTS

In 1892, Francis Galton calculated that the chances of two people having the same fingerprints were one in 64 billion. That same year, Argentine police officer Juan Vucetich used fingerprints to identify a murderer. Vucetich also created the world's first "fingerprint bureau." Police forces around the world soon did the same.

BLOOD

Human blood types were first discovered in 1900. A year later, they were used for the first time in Germany. Scientists worked out that blood on Ludwig Tessnow's shirt was human, not animal as he claimed. This helped to convict him of killing two people.

DNA

Left-behind DNA first led to a criminal conviction for murder in 1987. Colin Pitchfork at first tried to avoid taking a DNA test by getting a friend to take it instead. When police discovered this, they did the test—and found that it matched evidence from the crime scene.

A crime-scene investigator collects blood samples.

Geneticist

Have you ever wondered why some people have red hair, others blonde? Or maybe why children often look like their parents? If unlocking the answer to how a living organism looks and behaves sounds interesting, you might enjoy being a geneticist.

BIO-TESTERS

Geneticists are scientists of biology. They do experiments to discover information about determinants, the ways in which characteristics pass from one generation to the next. Many of these characteristics are passed on through DNA, which contains instructions on how a living thing should look and behave, called a "genetic code." The characteristics could be visible things, such as hair color, or invisible, such as characteristics that cause or prevent diseases. Geneticists may use this information to make improvements—for example, by developing crops that resist disease.

LAB INVESTIGATIONS

Geneticists work mainly in laboratories. There are lots of different kinds of jobs, depending on what most interests you. You could work in a hospital helping identify why patients are ill or which people are at risk of developing diseases. Drug companies use geneticists to help them develop new treatments. At an agricultural company, you might help develop new crops or other plants. At a university, you could be involved in cutting-edge research.

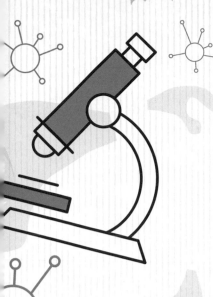

STEM STARS: FRANKLIN, WILKINS, WATSON, AND CRICK

FRANKLIN (1920-1958)
WILKINS (1916-2004)
WATSON (1928-)
CRICK (1916-2004)

Francis Crick

James Watson

In 1962, Maurice Wilkins, Francis Crick, and James Watson won the Nobel Prize for Medicine. They were awarded the prize for their work in discovering the structure of DNA. Missing from the prizewinners was Rosalind Franklin, who had worked alongside Wilkins. Franklin had died in 1958. Her experimental work had been crucial to the discovery, but the prize could not be awarded to her after her death.

Brain surgeon

How the human brain works is one of the biggest mysteries on Earth. There are many things that we do not fully understand about the brain, but scientists do know which parts do which jobs and understand much of its complicated structure. When something goes wrong, a specially skilled surgeon is needed to fix it.

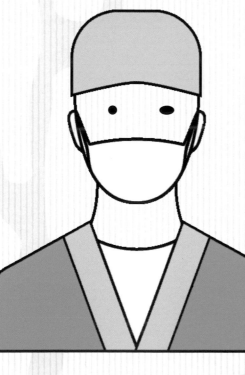

STEADY HANDS

Brain surgery starts off with getting through the patient's skull. The skull is made of thick bone to help prevent the brain being injured. Getting through it is not easy. Drills and saws are used, so brain surgeons cannot be squeamish. Once exposed, the brain is very delicate, so brain surgeons need steady hands. One shake or slip could be disastrous.

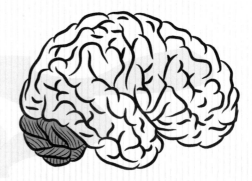

TOOLS OF THE TRADE

Brain surgery requires specialist tools, usually for either cutting, clamping shut, or holding in place. Most have been in existence for decades, but recently robots and computer software have been added to the brain surgeon's toolkit. The exact tools a surgeon uses depend on the kind of surgery he or she specializes in. Some surgeons cut out life-threatening growths called tumors. Others stop blood vessels from leaking, try to fix problems, such as epilepsy, or repair injury damage.

TRAINING: SIMULATION SURGERY

Simulators, machines that create a lifelike experience, can be used to help surgeons practice a robot operation. Images of the patient's brain are taken and used to create an on-screen model. The surgeon can practice the operation, using the same tools to guide the robot as in the actual operation.

A brain surgeon at work on the operating table. ⋯⋯⋯

Nanotechnologist

Some people are interested in big things, such as monster trucks or giant skyscrapers. Other people find tiny objects fascinating: little cogs in a watch, miniature radios, or microscopic animals. If you're interested in tiny objects, nanotechnology might have a job for you.

NANO WHAT?

A nanometer is a tiny measure of length (a thin sheet of paper is about 100,000 nanometers thick). Nanotechnologists work with some of the smallest objects we can see, even with a microscope. In fact, the microscopes used to see nanotechnology were only invented about 35 years ago. Nanotechnologists use all kinds of science as well as engineering and digital technology.

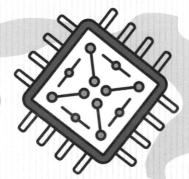

LAB TIME

Most of a nanotechnologist's work is done in a laboratory. There are lots of different kinds of nanotechnology, so there are all kinds of different things you could be working on. Imagine working on nano-robots that can travel through someone's blood and cure diseases. How would they get there? Could tiny viruses carry them? Which one works best? Finding out could be your job. Or you could be setting up an experiment for a new sunscreen, which contains nanoparticles that reflect or absorb dangerous radiation.

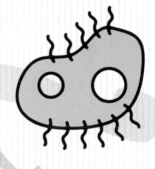

STEM STAR: K. ERIC DREXLER (1955–)

Drexler is sometimes called one of the founding fathers of nanotechnology. His ideas have influenced the development of this science since the 1980s. Drexler was not the first person to use the actual word "nanotechnology," though; that was invented by Norio Taniguchi (1912–1999) in 1974.

Paleontologist

Millions of year ago, Earth was warmer and the atmosphere was different. The land itself was a different shape and huge reptiles ruled. If you like the idea of discovering what the planet was like back then, perhaps you should become a paleontologist.

FOSSIL FASCINATION

Experts think that 99 percent of all species to have ever lived are now extinct. Some left behind remains called fossils. Being a paleontologist is all about fossils. You will dig them up, decide what kind of plant or animal they are from, and then work out as much information as possible about how the plant or animal lived.

Amber, which is fossilized resin from a tree, contains tiny air bubbles from millions of years ago. Paleontologists study any gases in the bubbles to find out what the atmosphere was like back then.

One-seventh of all the dinosaurs we know about were found in Mongolia. Bolortsetseg Minjin has discovered hundreds of dinosaur fossils in the deserts of Mongolia. In 2007, she established the Institute for the Study of Mongolian Dinosaurs to help Mongolians learn about these fossils and to train paleontologists. She also tours schools to teach children about her country's rich fossil record.

SOMETHING FOR EVERYONE

Whatever it is about the ancient past that fascinates you, there will be a kind of paleontology for it. Some paleontologists study a particular kind of animal, dinosaurs from the *Tyrannosaurus* genus, for example. Others specialize in the tiniest creatures, such as bacteria. The three major kinds of paleontologists are:

1) People who study invertebrates, animals without a backbone
2) Experts in vertebrate animals, which do have a backbone
3) Those who study plants, who are sometimes called paleobotanists.

Behind the scenes:
Dinosaur digs

The most famous area of paleontology is research into dinosaurs. At the moment, about one new dinosaur species is being discovered every week. The hotspots for dinosaurs are at digs in China, Mongolia, and Argentina, huge countries that famous paleontologist Stephen Brusatte says are "full of rocks bursting with dinosaur bones."

CHINA

About half of the new dinosaurs being discovered are in China. Some of the discoveries are changing how we think about dinosaurs. In 2017, for example, *Halszkaraptor escuilliei* was unearthed. The fossil was scanned while still contained in rock, to avoid damaging it. The scan revealed a dinosaur that looks more like a modern-day swan than a traditional reptilelike animal.

MONGOLIA

In 2017, paleontologist Buuvei Mainbayar uncovered a backbone in the Gobi Desert. He sent it to his team leader, Takanobu Tsuihiki, who recognized that it came from a pterosaur—one of the flying reptiles of the dinosaur era. He said, "I was astonished at its gigantic size. Straight away, we went back to the site and discovered the rest of the specimen." It turned out to be a pterosaur as big as *Quetzalcoatlus*, the largest of the pterosaurs.

ARGENTINA

In Argentina, paleontologists unearthed a new dinosaur they named *Ingentia prima*, which means "first giant." This dinosaur weighed about 11 tons (10 mt) and is the earliest giant dinosaur we know about. Other famous giants, such as *Diplodocus* and *Brachiosaurus*, appeared about 30 million years later. Scientists analyzed *Ingentia*'s bones and found growth rings (a bit like the growth rings in a tree trunk), which showed it had experienced huge growth spurts to reach its size quickly.

Digging up dinosaur bones must be done very carefully.

23

Carbon-dating scientist

The last ice age ended 11,700 years ago. Scotland's Orkney Islands were first settled 5,600 years ago. The Maya civilization of Central America collapsed in the year 200 CE and again in 900 CE. But how do we know all this? It's because of the work done by carbon-dating scientists.

AGING ANYTHING

Carbon-dating scientists work out the age of things that were once a plant or animal. All living things contain a chemical called carbon 14. As soon as they die, plants and animals stop taking in carbon 14 and the amount contained in their body begins to decrease. By measuring the amount left behind, scientists can work out how long ago the plant or animal died.

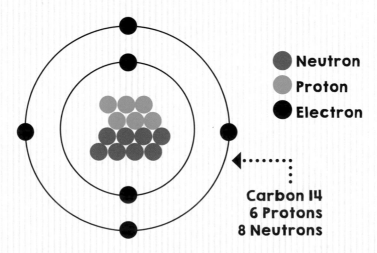

Neutron
Proton
Electron

Carbon 14
6 Protons
8 Neutrons

ARCHAEOLOGICAL ARTIFACTS

As a carbon-dating scientist, one of your main areas of work would be archaeology. For example, imagine an ancient sword has been dug up. How old is it? You date the wooden box the sword was inside, giving the archaeologists a valuable clue to its age. Carbon dating has also been used to work out when ancient papers were written, when pieces of cloth were made, and the age of old pottery and pieces of bone.

STEM STAR:
WILLARD LIBBY
(1908–1980)

Libby worked on the Manhattan Project, which built the first nuclear weapons during the Second World War (1939–45). He invented carbon dating in the 1940s and also developed a similar process for dating water. In 1960 Libby won the Nobel Prize for Chemistry, in recognition of his work.

Particle physicist

What is dark matter? In fact, have you even heard of dark matter? If you have, you probably also know: a) no one really has much idea what dark matter is because we can't see it and b) if anyone does find out, it will be a particle physicist who makes the discovery.

SMASHING JOB

As a particle physicist, your job will be investigating particles (which probably doesn't come as a surprise). Particles are smaller than atoms; they are the tiniest pieces of which objects are made. Particle physicists dream of finding new ones. One of the main ways of doing this is to smash matter together in a machine called a collider and record what happens as a result.

TESTING IDEAS

There are two main types of particle physicists: theoretical and experimental. The experimental scientists are the ones who get to smash things. (There is actually more to the job than this, measuring, recording, and understanding the results, for example.) The theoretical scientists develop mathematical theories to describe the results of the experiments. This mathematics is used to predict new results from different experiments. These new experiments are then performed as a way of testing the theories.

STEM STAR: RICHARD FEYNMAN (1918–1988)

Feynman was a mathematician and physicist who helped develop the quantum theory that particle physicists explore today. His best-selling book *Surely You're Joking, Mr. Feynman!* describes not only his work in physics, but also his fascination with safecracking, playing the bongo drums in a band, and other fun stories.

Behind the scenes:
Colliders and accelerators

Imagine telling your grandma that you got a job at the " Large Hadron Collider" or (maybe an even better name) the "Relativistic Heavy Ion Collider." She would definitely feel proud of you! Those are two of the most famous places where particle physicists work.

CERN

(Geneva, Switzerland)

The Large Hadron Collider is at the European Organization for Nuclear Research (CERN). Almost 8,000 scientists and engineers work here. The collider is a loop of powerful magnets 17 miles (27 km) long. Inside, two particle beams travel in opposite directions, reaching almost the speed of light before they smash together. The two beams are very narrow, so getting them to collide is not easy. In fact, it is like firing two needles at each other from several miles apart and making their points hit each other.

The Large Hadron Collider at CERN, Switzerland ⋯

Relativistic Heavy Ion Collider at Brookhaven National Laboratory

(Long Island, USA)

There are jobs for about 3,000 scientists, engineers, technicians, and support staff at Brookhaven National Laboratory. As well as this, the laboratory is used by about 4,000 guest researchers each year. The Relativistic Heavy Ion Collider is the world's second-biggest and most powerful particle accelerator. Scientists can use it to study the form of matter that existed just after the Big Bang, when the universe began to form.

KEK High-Energy Accelerator Research Organization

(Tsukuba, Japan)

There are almost 700 scientists and others working at KEK, as well as visiting researchers from other organizations. One of its leading scientists, Makoto Kobayashi, won the 2008 Nobel Prize for physics. It was for "the discovery of the origin of broken symmetry, which predicts the existence of at least three families of quarks in nature." If you understood that, you're probably already a particle physicist.

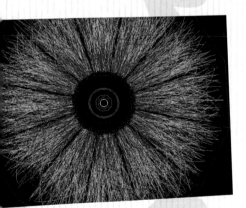

Two gold ions collide with dramatic results!

Sports scientist

In sports, some people can run faster, compete for longer, or develop skills more quickly than others. But what is it that makes this so? If the idea of unlocking the secrets of sports success sounds interesting, you might enjoy working as a sports scientist.

SPORTS STUDIES

Sports scientists study how the human body—including the brain—works during sports. They use a wide range of tools. These include video analysis, taking a video and then playing it back in slow motion, to spot tiny mistakes in technique. Sports scientists also use blood and oxygen tests to work out what is going on inside an athlete.

GETTING BETTER

If you become a sports scientist, there are lots of different types of jobs out there. At universities, sports scientists do research. Imagine, for example, helping the army to develop new tests to assess the fitness of recruits. At a sports organization, the sports scientists might help the team develop better training methods, improve skills, or help athletes prevent or recover from injury. You could even specialize in sports psychology: the way an athlete's mind can affect their performance in a game or competition.

TRAINING:
MIND OVER MATTER

Steve Peters is a famous sports psychologist from England. He has worked for cycling, rugby, tae kwon do, and other kinds of sports teams. Peters's most famous idea is the "inner chimp"—his way of describing emotional thinking, which can stop athletes performing at their absolute best.

A sports scientist collects and studies ·········▶ performance data.

Oceanographer

Oceans cover just over 70 percent of our planet. They range from the icy seas of the polar regions to the warm waters of the tropics. The oceans contain a huge variety of life, including tiny plankton and the largest creature on Earth—the blue whale. Oceanographers study all of this.

LIFE ON THE OCEAN WAVES

If you don't like swimming or being on a boat, this might not be the best science job for you. Fieldwork—seeing what happens in real life, rather than in a laboratory—is a crucial part of an oceanographer's job. One day you might be journeying below the waves wearing scuba gear. Another you might be recording deep-ocean currents in the Arctic.

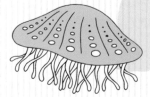

SYLVIA EARLE
(1935-)

Sylvia Earle is an oceanographer. She has led over 100 expeditions and spent over 41 weeks of her life underwater (not all at once). She was the first female chief scientist at the U.S. National Oceanographic and Atmospheric Administration, and in 1998 was *Time* magazine's first-ever Hero for the Planet.

OCEAN FASCINATION

There are many different specialist areas of oceanography, and thousands of subspecialties:

- Marine biologists study animals, plants, and their ecosystems.
- Physical oceanographers are interested in the ocean's waves, currents, and tides.
- Chemical oceanographers study the chemicals found in the water, including any pollution.
- Geological oceanographers study the ocean floor, including undersea volcanic activity.

Many oceanographic discoveries are made by teams of scientists from different specialties working together.

Meteorologist

There are lots of old sayings about the weather, and none of them are 100 percent accurate. Although, it is possible to spot clues in the world around us, which might help predict what the weather might do next. If you would prefer a more reliable way to predict the weather, think about becoming a weather forecaster.

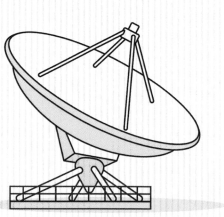

FORECASTING

Some meteorologists specialize in forecasting. They try to predict the weather, which is useful for all kinds of people: farmers who need to know when to plant and harvest crops; people at sea who need to know if dangerous conditions are coming; and people going about their ordinary lives. Forecasters use information from satellite images, radar, and weather stations. Their computer models make short-range and long-range weather forecasts.

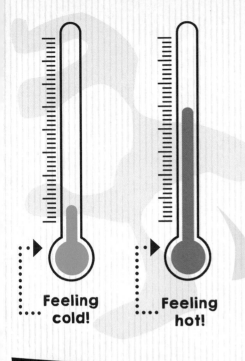

Feeling cold!

Feeling hot!

WEATHER RESEARCH

Weather researchers are meteorologists who investigate how weather patterns work and how the climate is changing. Their research is used to develop and improve computer weather forecasting systems. Research meteorologists also try to solve practical problems. These include working out the risks of flooding or coastal erosion getting worse, how river flooding can be predicted, and even how the weather affects the spread of pollution or disease.

TRAINING:
TV WEATHER FORECASTER

Most TV weather broadcasters are trained meteorologists, though some are expert presenters who learn about meteorology later. Before doing live broadcasts, they are trained in pointing to the weather map without looking at it, using a teleprompter, and talking while someone is speaking to them through an earpiece.

Weather broadcasters have to be skilled at thinking on their feet!

Scientific photographer

If you have a smartphone with a camera on it, call up your photo gallery. Does it show unusual views, different angles, extreme close-ups, and subjects no one else has taken? If so, maybe you could be a scientific photographer.

DATA IN DETAIL

Scientific photographers use advanced photographic techniques and equipment to record scientific data. They use infrared and ultraviolet photography, time-lapse, microscopic photography, and many other techniques to record science data. Often their photos show things that cannot normally be seen. A scientific photographer has to understand what they are photographing and why, so you need to be interested in science and photography to do this job.

HI-TECH VIEWS

Some scientific photographers specialize in a particular area of work. This usually develops from the subject they know most about: biology, chemistry, medicine, or engineering, for example. You could end up taking microscopic photos of how metals or concrete behave under stress. In medical research, you might spend days taking photos of bacteria, or in a laboratory, you could be capturing images of the tiniest particles that can be seen with a microscope.

STEM STAR: FELICE FRANKEL
(1945–)

The best scientific photographers make images that are not only scientific but also beautiful to look at. Frankel is famous for her beautiful photos that reveal details too small for our eyes to see, such as the close-up details of a butterfly's wing or patterns of nanocrystals. She works at the world-famous Massachusetts Institute of Technology (MIT), where she is the scientific photographer. Her book *Picturing Science and Engineering* contains many of her best-known images.

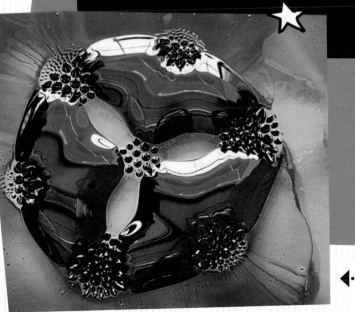

◀····· **Frankel's photograph of a magnetized liquid called ferrofluid.**

Behind the scenes:
Science in extreme worlds

When people hear the word "scientist," they often think of white lab coats and test tubes. But science happens everywhere, not only in laboratories. While you are reading this, there are scientists working in some of our planet's most extreme environments – and beyond.

UNDER THE VOLCANO

Scientists called volcanologists work in the shadow of volcanoes to understand how they behave and whether they are likely to erupt. The world's major volcanoes— Mount Etna in Italy, Rainier in the United States, and Popocatépetl in Mexico, for example—are constantly monitored. This is not a safe job: volcanologists have been killed by volcanic activity.

BENEATH EARTH'S SURFACE

One science few people have heard of is speleology, the study of caves. Speleologists study how caves are formed, their climates, and the animals and plants that live in them. To do this, they have to travel underground (sometimes deep below ground), through narrow passages, and to places that can be cut off by rising water in a cave system.

POLAR RESEARCH

The North and South Poles are among the most difficult places on Earth to live. The temperature is below freezing for weeks, winds of over 100 miles (160 km) per hour blow, and no plants grow. Only the most specialized animals can survive here—humans can only survive by wearing special clothing. Even so, scientists spend months living in Arctic and Antarctic research stations, studying the climate, atmosphere, and natural world.

SPACE

Space must be the most extreme environment of all. There isn't even air to breathe up there, unless you bring it with you. Space scientists live in small spaces where zero gravity makes almost everything more complicated than on Earth. They study the effects of zero gravity on humans and other living creatures.

Astronauts aboard the International Space Station

Climate scientist

Everyone notices when it's a sunny day or a rainy one. They are noticing the weather. But if you notice that it is unusually warm and sunny on a winter's day, then you are noticing something different in the climate. Maybe being a climate scientist would be a good job for you.

TOOLS OF THE TRADE

Climate scientists rely on all kinds of instruments. Rain gauges measure how much rain has fallen. Barometers show air pressure, thermometers record the temperature, and hygrometers show how much moisture there is in the air. Climate scientists feed data from their instruments into computer programs, which build a bigger picture of how the climate works and ways it is changing.

A weather station with many instruments

Solar panels capture data about levels of sunshine

CLIMATE EVERYWHERE

Working as a climate scientist could take you all over the world. You might find yourself drilling down into the ice of a glacier or looking for bubbles of air trapped in the ice thousands of years ago. You may end up in the middle of a forest, examining tree rings to find out what the climate was like as the tree grew. Or you could be on a boat in the Pacific Ocean, investigating how a climate event called El Niño has affected marine life.

STEM STAR: SUSAN SOLOMON (1956–)

Solomon specializes in atmospheric chemistry. In the 1970s, holes appeared in the layer of gas called ozone above Earth's poles. Ozone protects the world from dangerous radiation, so this was serious. Solomon realized that the holes were caused by chemicals called CFCs, which were used in most refrigerators. As a result, CFCs were phased out at the end of the 20th century and the use of CFCs for manufacturing is now illegal.

Food scientist

Are you the one in your family who checks food containers to see how fresh the ingredients are inside? Or maybe you like tracking the growth of mold on an old bit of bread? If so, you might just have the makings of a food scientist.

NEW TASTES, NEW FLAVORS

One of your jobs might be to understand which chemicals in different foods make people like or dislike them. This knowledge could be used to design new foods (or drinks)—ones that people really enjoy. Imagine inventing a cabbage that tastes like ice cream!

EVERYTHING FOOD

As a food scientist, you might use your scientific training to study food in lots of different ways. You could be working out when the use-by date should be or how to keep food fresh for as long as possible. Working out the nutritional value of foods and whether they have been produced in a safe way are important jobs. So are checking foods for harmful mold or bacteria and trying to develop new kinds of food.

STEM STAR:
M. S. SWAMINATHAN
(1925–)

Swaminathan is famous for his leading role in India's Green Revolution, which introduced modern farming methods to the country. He helped develop new kinds of wheat that had more grains and stronger stalks to hold the heavy grains. Introducing these new crop varieties to farmers allowed them to grow more food for India's growing population.

Behind the scenes:
Food for the future

The world's population grows each year, which means we need more food than ever before. Scientists around the world are working to make sure we have enough food to keep the population fed and healthy.

FOOD GENES

Modern farming produces a lot of food, but it does not always contain a lot of nutrition. In fact, today's vegetables have only about 66 percent as many minerals as 100 years ago. Scientists are working to improve this situation. They take genetic code from a plant that naturally has high levels of a particular nutrient. The code is added to a similar plant, which then develops higher levels of the nutrient.

PERSONALIZED NUTRITION

Scientists are beginning to understand that the same foods affect people differently. One person might get a sudden spike in energy from ice cream, for example, while another doesn't. The second person might get an energy spike from rice instead. Scientists can use DNA testing to work out which foods are best for individuals and which ones they should avoid.

NASA FOOD LAB

The NASA food lab is busy developing, processing, and packaging food for space flights. There is no refrigeration in space, and the food has to be ready to eat, heat, or rehydrate. It also has to last for a long time. The lab is working on foods that will stay fresh enough for a two-and-a-half-year flight to Mars and back. NASA's food scientists report that astronauts' current favorite meals are spicy food, tortillas, and shrimp cocktail. This may be because their sense of taste is less sensitive when living in space.

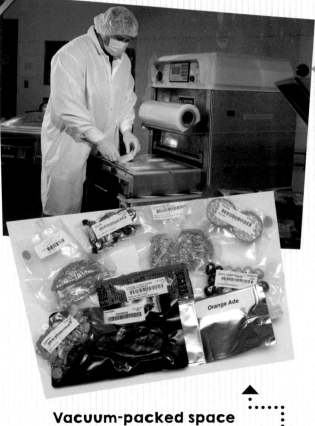

Vacuum-packed space food can last for years.

Glossary

atmosphere
layer of gases surrounding Earth (or any other moon or planet)

atom
tiny unit of matter, made up of a core (or nucleus) of neutrons and protons surrounded by a cloud of electrons

Big Bang
massive, extremely fast explosion of matter that started the formation of the universe

clamping
holding together using a clamp, which is a bit like a clothes-pin that can be tightened or loosed

collider
in physics, a collider is a device for forcing tiny particles to collide at high speed

communications
exchanging information, usually by speaking or writing. For space travel to and from the International Space Station (ISS), astronauts need to know enough Russian to communicate aboard the Russian Soyuz craft that travels between Earth and the ISS.

determinants
genetic triggers that cause characteristics, such as appearance, to be passed from one generation to the next

dig
in archaeology and paleontology, a dig is an exploration of what lies beneath the surface of the soil. Each layer of soil or rock is carefully removed to see if it contains evidence from the past.

docking
in space travel, docking is when two spacecraft move together and then link, usually so that passengers can move from one to the other

ecosystem
community of living things, plants and animals, that are all adapted to live in a particular place. The term "ecosystem" also includes the place itself.

fieldwork
in science, fieldwork is research that is done out in the world (such as in a desert, under the ocean, in space, or at the poles), rather than in an office or laboratory

forensics
using science to investigate a crime

fossil
remains of a prehistoric plant or animal that have been embedded in rock. Many fossils are millions of years old.

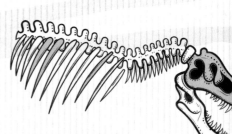